For Andrea

DEREK

For Thomas and Martin

JOHN

Text copyright © 1985 by Derek Hall
Illustrations copyright © 1985 by John Butler
All rights reserved under International and Pan-American Copyright
Conventions. Published in the United States by Alfred A. Knopf, Inc.,
New York. Distributed by Random House, Inc., New York.
Originally published in Great Britain by Walker Books Ltd., London
Manufactured in Italy   10 9 8 7 6 5 4 3 2 1
First American Edition

Library of Congress Cataloging in Publication Data
Hall, Derek, 1930-   Gorilla builds. (Growing up)
Summary: Baby Gorilla takes a tumble and learns the importance of
building her nest in a strong tree.
1. Gorillas – Juvenile literature.   [1. Gorillas]
I. Butler, John, 1952-   , ill.   II. Title.
III. Series: Growing up (Alfred A. Knopf)
QL737.P96H35   1985   599.88'46   84-25107
ISBN 0-394-86530-8   ISBN 0-394-96530-2 (lib. bdg.)

Gorilla Builds

By Derek Hall

Illustrations by John Butler

Sierra Club / Alfred A. Knopf

San Francisco   New York

Gorilla and her father finish their dinner in the forest. She has eaten lots of tasty leaves. He likes to chew on juicy stalks as well.

Gorilla's father is sleepy and decides to make a nest. He bends stalks and leaves over and treads on them until they are soft. Gorilla watches.

Her father settles back on
the nest, wriggling around and
stretching until he is comfortable.
Poor Gorilla – there's no room
for her!

Gorilla decides to make her
own nest. She climbs a tree near
her father and rocks backwards
and forwards on it. It's fun –
it's like a swing.

But Gorilla is a bit too heavy.
And the tree is a bit too thin.
It suddenly bends right over and
Gorilla slips. She is falling . . .

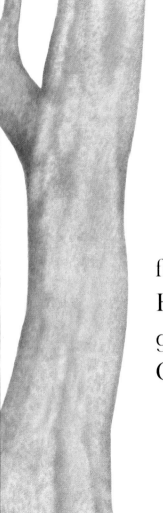

She lands on top of her
father and wakes him up.
He scrambles to his feet,
grumpy and grumbling.
Gorilla hurries away.

Gorilla climbs a stronger tree.
She bends leafy twigs and branches
over. Then she tramples on them
to make a soft cushion of leaves.

Gorilla has done it – made
her first nest high up in a tree!
She snuggles down and nibbles
some more leaves. Gorilla feels
just like a grownup.